For Mom & Dad —

Happy Anniversary.

Love,

Tall
Houses

Tall
Houses

By

ELIZABETH VERNER HAMILTON

and

LOUISE FRIERSON KERR

TRADD STREET PRESS

Charleston, South Carolina

1981

Printed by
Nelsons' Southern Printing Company
Charleston, South Carolina

DEDICATED

TO

CHARLESTON

ACKNOWLEDGMENTS

Some of the poems have appeared in the *Junior League Magazine*. Others have been published by *Cobblestones*, the news sheet of The Charleston Junior League. We made a deliberate attempt to portray Charlestonians living and dead. We hope these tributes will be accepted in the loving spirit in which they are offered.

L. F. K. - E. V. H.

CONTENTS

CONTENTS—*Continued*

*Tall
Houses*

The gate is iron fashioned into lace;
Beside it stands a sign, discreet and small,
To bid us welcome to the tiny place
Ablaze with Spring behind the ancient wall.
The flagstones, laid in careful patterned line,
Are bordered by the little formal beds
Adorned with hyacinths, and jonquils shine
Like gold beside the graceful tulip heads.
A waxy late camellia touches groups
Of lavish flame azaleas. All the air
Is quick with fragrance, — from the loops
Of jessamine, wistaria, and where
The Lady Banksia pours its loveliness.
All Nature waits us here in formal dress.

L. F. K.

1

Walls

I used to think,
A long, long time ago,
That all about the walls,
Between the floors,
Were little secret rooms
And tiny passages,
Built in some forgotten age
When men believed there were such things
As goblins.

I knew that in the garden,
Back behind the wall,
A hundred little city gnomes
Kept house,
Twisted beings
With the wisdom of the ages
In their eyes.
I used to see them there
Sometimes.

But now I know,
Since I've looked far and wide
And everywhere such solid building found,
That those forgotten men,
Although they builded well,
Were only building
Walls.

E. V. H.

Down the narrow street
I hear more than the beat
Of my hurrying feet.

Church
Street

Antique patterns tracing
Running, walking, pacing,
I am replacing whom
Long gone to the tomb?

I'll go, just as I came,
While Charlestonians still
Whose names
I'll never know,
Will
Hear my own
Echo —
Different —
But the same.

E. V. H.

3

William
Mason
Smith

of
Church
Street

He's eighty-eight and luminous;
He's eighty-eight and very wise.
Wisdom shines through fine-drawn lines
And twinkles in his eyes.

He's eighty-eight and humorous;
He's eighty-eight and gently kind.
His forebears learned this self-restraint
We see as peace of mind.

E. V. H.

4

Tall Houses

The tall old houses stand together
And brace themselves against the weather.
Some have erratic stands
Like piles of flotsam drifted—
While some, by alien hands,
Have had their faces lifted.

The tall old houses like the feeling
Of gulls around their chimneys wheeling.
Their shuttered eyes unclose
As gentle vernal breezes
Disturb their dust's repose,
Inducing human sneezes.

The tall old houses, standing primly,
View strangers with suspicion, grimly.
Toward visitors with tact
And bearing meek and lowly
They soften, though in fact
They don't accept them wholly.

The tall old houses, gently smiling
With welcome full of warm beguiling,
Take back into the brood,
With tender murmured rustles,
The wanderer whose blood
Has Charleston's blue corpuscles.

L. F. K.

Susan Pringle Frost

Her native city knew her as Miss Sue;
They smiled at her persistence, yet respect
Marked their address of her because they knew,
Without her burning ardor to protect,
The treasure bounded by the ancient lines
Would vanish from the memory of man,
And all of Charleston's heirs and her assigns
Would soon forget the way the legend ran.
The tall old houses, with their mellow walls
And slanted windows set by cheerful hand,
Their lofty-ceilinged rooms and spacious halls,
Because of her concern, still proudly stand.
To save the town she loved, her life was spent.
The living city is her monument.

L. F. K.

Grande
Dame

No passive voice—
Imperatives, she uses
Richly. Her choice of words amuses.
Her velvet timbre
Can dismember
The pretentious mind,
But she is not unkind.

E. V. H.

Portrait

of an

Old

Lady

Her skin is like
Rose petals soaked by rain
And beaten by a storm
Against a window pane.

Her hair is gathered
Spider webs, fine-spun,
Combed and silvered
Each hair, one by one.

And life long running through her veins
Has carried off all dross
And left a spirit freed, that counts
Her eighty years no loss.

E. V. H.

To be posted in the Manigault House

Nell
Pringle
Speaks

Do not forget me.
I put my heart into this house.
It was defeated, doomed,
To be demolished.
All crinolines gone,
All wigs and pantaloons
Packed in trunks
And then thrown out.
And no one to come again,
In powdered curls and snowy frill,
To stand in front
Of tall gilt mirrors,
Lit by candlelight;
To talk of
Justice and the country's weal.

Four families crowded to a floor,
Wainscoting ripped
And stair-rails burned,
Adam mantels hidden
Deep in grime,
Awaiting the bulldozer's demolition.

I, Nell Pringle, saved it.
I signed the note
For Preservation.
Ahead of my time, I was;
Voices were raised in support
But echoed fruitlessly.

I saved this house!

E. V. H.

9

Flower

Mart

Across from staid Saint Michael's Church
Mad color riots, swoops and swirls,
Where, on the curb and sidewalk, perch
A swarm of Charleston flower girls.

Perfumed azaleas, wild and tame,
Against the glossed magnolia leaves,
Blaze white and purple, pink and flame,
While pale swamp ladies stand in sheaves.

Forsythia, peach-blossoms, too,
Snapdragons, stock and jonquils sing.
Rich voices cry their wares to you;
Dark hands are offering you the Spring.

Two bunches for a quarter, Miss!
Oh, Miss, please buy my flowers, do!
Yes, Ma'am, I got some more of this—
I got some yalla jess'mine, too!

Dark faces ring you like a fence,
Importunate with smiling charm;
And if you squander fifty cents
For ten cents' value, where's the harm?

L. F. K.

In
St. Philip's
Churchyard

Here sleeps the dead. How peacefully she lies
Below the covering earth,
Awaiting her new birth,
Quietly she lies
Beneath the quiet skies.

On her ebon casket, glossy-smooth and fine,
There were silver handles.
At her feet, life's candles
Ever seemed to shine.
She drank life like wine.

Like rare wine the perfume of the blooming rose,
From the rich earth springing.
Can you hear her singing
As the flower blows?
On her heart it grows,—

Exquisite, the essence of her daintiness,
Yet the plant is strong,
Young as she was young.
In this altered dress,
Is she then the less?

L. F. K.

11

Epitaph
for
Louisa

Here lies one who gave so much
Of gaiety and love
That people brought their hearts to her
As empty cups for filling.

L. F. K.

*A Visit by
Eda Noel
to Certain
Ladies
Living
in Close
Retirement*

Ah! Strange that she should be here speaking so!
Be here in this drab room where, stiff with dust,
Propriety is crabbed with age and must;
That she should speak of Cannes and Borneo,
Rio, the Amazon and Scotch Glasgow
And Swaziland—to us who ever thrust
Impulse aside and scorned the wanderlust.
Her magic voice brings here a shifting show,
Carved ivory chairs and curious golden sleeves,
Old tapestries; in vibrant tones, it weaves
Delight, and we who listen shall not weep
While dull, drab days drag by, this room shall keep
The echo of her accents clear and strong
As morning echoes with the thrushes' song.

E. V. H.

They say when Dr. Steinberg died
All the colored people cried.
The funeral parlor all day long
Was filled with their grief-stricken song,
Such spirituals as one seldom hears
In these media-ridden years.
And I was very glad to find
That he had thus served mankind.

He was in my German class;
I was a fluffy-minded lass,
And once in rage he turned his head
And with the utmost scorn he said;
Why can't you see!
'E–i' is 'i', 'i–e' is 'e'!

And of course it was unfair
That I should breathe the self-same air
And make the class-room work so slow
When he had so far to go.

E. V. H.

College of
Charleston

Doctor's Office

The house is old. No casual passerby
Who might, in thoughtless ignorance, deplore
The gardens where azaleas bloom no more,
Would know of lives renewed, though flowers die.
Within, the ceilings in the rooms are high,
Long windows reach the ceiling from the floor.
Street sounds are muffled by the massive door
Which closes slowly with a creaking sigh.
The rugs are worn where many feet have trod;
The dog-eared books incline, a huddled pile,
On old mahogany. The polished fender rod
Gives back the shimmer of the fire, while
Each worried patient waits the nurse's nod
Then, quick with hope, reflects the doctor's smile.

L. F. K.

Fire
Engines

Whipped the wind
Down the narrow street.
Sirens whined.
Paper blew against our feet.
From sound there is no retreat.

The sirens whined.
Uneasy our hearts beat;
The very mind
Howled with the menacing bleat.
From city sounds there is no retreat.

E. V. H.

16

The
Shattered
Mirror

Today the paper tells me he has died,
The last of all the men who loved me true.
While he was here to praise it, I descried
Faint traces of the beauty I once knew.
I wore the special colors that were mine;
Arranged my hair the most becoming way,
And had my rich rewarding in the shine
Of his admiring eyes and heard him say,
You're just as lovely as you ever were!
He made me feel so treasured, I would smile,
Secure within the knowledge I could stir
Warm embers into flame in just a while.
Now I face age and ugliness alone.
My beauty vanished when his eyes were gone.

L. F. K.

Bald
Cypress

In swamps the great bald cypress grow.
Their roots, upthrust, are old men's knees.
Around them, sluggish waters flow.

Hot summer drains the swamplands low
And leaves are withered in the breeze.
In buttressed strength the cypress grow.

There are moccasins, you know,
In tangled vines between the trees;
Around them sluggish waters flow.

Wintry winds and high gales blow;
The blackened waters chill and freeze;
Impervious the cypress grow.

But in the Spring, the flowers glow,
While languid herons flit at ease;
Like mighty piers the cypress grow
And bright reflecting waters flow.

E. V. H.

The tide is flowing in and dolphins leap
Against the golden backdrop of the marsh
She loved to paint. All sounds are soft, no harsh
Discordance mars the sunset hour. Sweep
On sweep of color stains the evening sky.
Above the river glints a flash of white,
Two herons winging nestward for the night.
The half-ring of the baby moon is high.
With such perfection she portrayed these things
That they became peculiarly her own
And cypress-filtered sunlight still is known
As Alice R. H. Smith's,—the brush that sings.
Prodigious genius in that tiny frame
Made art of life and life a joyous game.

*Alice
Ravenel
Huger
Smith*

L. F. K.

The Charleston Lady

You'll find, in travelling far abroad,
In drawing-rooms or gardens shady,
No ornament unto the Lord
More charming than a Charleston lady.

A Charleston lady wears her hat,
Above her calm and smiling face,
Set straight upon her head,—like that!
And not a hair is out of place.

She never goes with ungloved hands;
She's always neat and simply dressed.
The most determined of commands
She phrases as a mild request.

A Charleston lady sits erect,—
She doesn't wave her hands about.
Her velvet voice is circumspect,
Yet more impressive than a shout.

Dismissing some officious boor,
To whom all courtesy is sham,
The quiet closing of her door
Has all the impact of a slam.

L. F. K.

Riding
on The
Island
The horses' hooves make a pattern of sound
(The continuum is the sea)—
Blue sky, gold sand, swift horse
Canter on to eternity.

E. V. H.

*Fort
Sumter
from
Sullivan's
Island*

Look across to Sumter, lying in the way,
Barring all intruders to the sheltered bay.
Listen! You can hear the voices of the guns!
Hear the Yankee's orders shouted as he runs
Through the narrow gauntlet, Moultrie on his right.
Watch the greening star-shells
      arching through the night.
Two grim years they held her, men and boys in gray,
Fighting, laughing, dying for Sumter in the way.
Now her guns are silent; on her battered walls
Children play and laugh with happy-hearted calls.
Never stand at evening on this lofty dune,
You will see her ramparts, with the rising moon,
Full of youthful shadows in Confederate gray;
Hear their ghostly voices from Sumter in the way.

                              L. F. K.

22

War
Memorial

Raise to them no shaft of stone
With a legend graven there,
They who sleep so far from home
Will not dream of it, nor care.

Japonicas and crimson quince,
Roses blooming new each year,
A garden is the evidence
Heroes are remembered here.

L. F. K.

Plum
Island

By favor of a gracious lady's hand,
We walked a narrow causeway years ago,
Preceded by the dancing, eager dog.
The tiny island waited in the sun,
A smiling welcome in the moving leaves
And straitened beaches rippled by the tide.
Above the narrow strand the ramparts rose,
Softened by time and garmented in trees
And grass, with blowing flowers. In the War
For Southern Independence (Civil War
To some), Confederate engineers dug out
The island's core and piled the earth in walls
Outside for breastworks, so to guard their home,
Their city, Charleston, on the other shore.
(She told us this. She was a Miss Huger,
The married one. Her name was Adger then.)
The place was stark and bared for grim defense
For war is ugly business and the scars
Are long in healing but the wind and rain
And sun, together with the marching years,
Brought beauty to Plum Island. There we strolled
And watched our puppy chasing butterflies.
We thanked the lady as we closed the gate.
Today my car traversed a broad causeway
And stopped upon a drab expanse of sand. . .
Some day the trees and grass may grow again
And frame once more the city's distant spires.

L. F. K.

24

Hurricane

First, there is quiet and the stifling heat
That weighs upon the body and the mind,—
No random breeze, no coolness to relieve
The breathless pressure.
Then a sudden gust
That whips the trees and bows the grass beneath
A dash of spitting rain,—then stillness and
The steaming heat again.
The wind is rising; gusts come oftener.
The rain beats now against the window-pane
And clouds are massing darkly in the sky.
The wind's low moan becomes a muted roar.
We leap to bolt the shutters and the door.
All fragile objects have been safely cached;
The candles, with their chimneys, are at hand,
The canned supplies, the sterno stove, the jars
And bottles filled with water.
So we wait
In our cocoon, alert to every change
Of mounting wind.
The tension builds. We listen to the shriek
Whose pitch sustained makes nerves a tuning fork
Until galvanic impulse, like the force
That draws the lightning from
    the surcharged clouds,
Propels us forth and sets us running in the streets,
Exulting in the fury of the storm.

L. F. K.

Spanish
Moss

Gray moss, quietly hanging there,
Stirring in vagrant air,
Veiling the trees,

Gold moss, veiling the agèd trees,
Sways with the elfin breeze,
Teasing the ground.

Smoke moss, teasing the waiting ground,
Flings its light tendrils 'round
Gnarled ancient limbs.

Mauve moss, swathing the ancient limbs
While the low sea-wind hymns,
Covers the leaves.

Taupe moss, covers the budding leaves,
While to its host it cleaves,
Creature of air.

Green moss, creature of light and air,
Feeding on atmosphere,
Pale epiphyte,

Gray moss, cool epiphyte, surrounds
Oaks in its filmy bounds,
Muffling the trees.

L. F. K.

Charleston:
A
Mosaic

This is a city of individuals.
Each person knows he is marked and unique.
Knowing himself, he is known of his fellows,
Names that are spoken have meaning for all.
Strange that this firm individualism,
That sets each apart from his neighbor, should fuse
Them in cohesiveness, firmly adhering,
Unique itself in a fragmented world.
When a life ends, in the closely knit city,
The gap that it leaves is ragged and torn.
No one who goes on ahead is forgotten;
His place is his own and can not be filled.
Those left behind are bleeding internally,
Feeling a part of themselves cut away.
With every parting, the whole is diminished;
None weeps alone for the whole city mourns.

L. F. K.

Samuel
Gaillard
Stoney

He knows the city like his facile hand
That writes, and gardens, carves enchanting things;
And he can give you stories, on demand,
Of cravens, heroes, commoners and kings.
His discourse is the opposite of terse.
With Charleston legends lilting on his lip,
And twinkling eye, he never is averse
To giving History an irreverent flip.
Behold him as he cycles through the streets,
With blowing grizzled beard and smiling eye,
And hear his booming laughter as he greets
Acquaintances among the passersby.
Though Samuel Gaillard Stoney is his name,
He's known as Mr. Charleston all the same.

l'envoi

Since this was written, Sam, our friend, has died
And left his city, shocked and stunned with grief
So deep and bitter, tears bring no relief.
Numb with pain, we mark the day, dry-eyed
Forever, in our somber memories.
Some men the city loves, he was of these.

L. F. K.

Cardinal
in the
Back
Yard

Scarlet-clad, he moves among the small brown flock,
Humble, unpresuming, kind.
He pecks at seeds companionably
And does not seem to realize
We've fed the greedy flock all year
To lure his August Presence here.

E. V. H.

Herbert
Ravenel
Sass

He wrote of Charleston and her history.
He loved the city and her characters,
The attributes that were uniquely hers—
Her grace, her strength, her deep integrity.
But most of all, he loved the rich, low land,
The singing marshes and the listening trees,
The birds—all birds. So great his love for these,
He could interpret calls and understand
Their motivation and their varied cries.
The bird *he* most resembled was the crane;
Tall, angular he was, with rufous mane,
With ready smile and blue, far-seeing eyes.
I cannot vouch for it but this I hear,
That, at his funeral, all the birds were there.

L. F. K.

Cattle Egrets

Black Angus cattle browse the distant meadow,
Design of polka dots against the green.
Near by each stocky form, his own attendant,
Awaits such insect largess he may glean.

How casual-seeming is the natural plan
That paints such contrast on the meadow's face:
The thick-legged, heavy body of the bull
Beside his snowy courtier's slender grace.

L. F. K.

Palmettoes

Tall sentinels,
What is the tune
Your pointed fingers
Play upon the wind?

E. V. H.

To

Yates

Snowden

The mark you made on every heart
That basked, though briefly,
And enhanced itself,
In your reflected charm,
Your swirling cape,
Your old felt hat, set rakishly a-tilt
Above your snowy mane!
(We would have lionized you
But our words
Fell limply down before the carte and tierce
Of your swift repartee).

L. F. K.

Portrait

Some called her homely. *What a sharp surprise*
To see in that plain face, they said, *those eyes!*
They said that she was mad.
Perhaps she was,
So fiercely to espouse another's cause.
She had a passion for justice,
Pushed and shoved
Against the walls of custom.
She was loved
Completely by the ones who knew her best;
Reviled and feared,—yes, hated
By the rest.
So deep was her compassion
She would know,
By instinct, of another's tortured woe
And take the burden of it on her own
Slim shoulders, there to carry it alone.

She suffered
Over everything in pain,
All wretched creatures in a world insane,
All frightened children,
All the desperate host
Of little people, desolate and lost.
Now she is gone,—I have forgotten where.
It doesn't matter. All I know is, there
She will be fighting still
Her ceaseless fight
Against brutality, with all her might.
What is she like? Why all that I recall
Is her intentness
And the drive and pull
Of single purpose through her nervous, small,
Slight figure. That is all.

L. F. K.

October Today the clear blue shadows
Dance wild dances in the sun;
And by the sea, the marsh-grass,
Rippling, plays chameleon.

E. V. H.

Harvest
Moon
Over
High
Battery

Let's write poetry
All in rhyme;
Let's sing songs
In fast time;
Let's slide down
Telegraph poles;
Let's run through
Rabbit holes.

E. V. H.

37

Departure

Yes, loving you, I now can go away
To live in any city, far or near,
That need or fate may take us to, nor fear
Insistent longing to return—by day.
But I will dream of houses on the bay;
Tall houses casting velvet shadows where
The shrimp man cries his catch, and vendors bear
Bright baskets on their heads, and children play.
But only promise this: when need is done,
I may return nor ever leave again
This city where the golden morning sun
Finds jewels in the dewdrops after rain,
And, while on misty nights the fog horn moans,
Old roots twist deep beneath the paving stones.

E. V. H.

The Night

How strange is the night. It scares me to think—
We shut out the dark, our little lights blink
In vastness of space. In spite of the blare
Of horns and fanfare in bright neon glare
Behind all the hoardings it's blacker than ink.
How strange is the night.

How still are the streets! Familiar walls sink
Into shadows. Houses are blind, not a chink
Of light there. If a child cried for care—!
How strange is the night!

One can open a door: there's no cat to slink
Out of sight. No! No movement at all. No drink
Eases the throbbing of waking nightmare.
The houses are empty! No one is there!
Day never will come! We have broken the link!
How strange is the night.

E. V. H.

Heritage

Before he went to his early grave
Judge Thomas Smith Grimké gave
A lecture
At the Old Scotch Church.
That was in 1828.
An education should, he said,
Prepare a man to use his head,
To think and to evaluate.
And this should be
For everyone
In a democracy.

And aren't his ideas current still
Under those copper domes?
I know they were, when I went there:
I've fought his battles everywhere,
Often under quite a strain—
Even with grandees in Spain.

E. V. H.

The King's Highway in Winter

Before us the road stretched broad and gray
And low overhead the gray sky lay.
Softly, it lay, as thistledown.
The trees were gray and the grass was brown
Save where the broomsedge widely spread
Its deep-piled carpet of tawny red.
I thought of many a sorrowful thing,
My heart like a bird with a trailing wing,
While the powerful motor swept us on.
We passed a barn, then a stream—both gone!
Until at last it began to seem
As though we sped through a waking dream,
Skirting a field's edge, topping a hill,
On through a dim wood, dreaming still.
A little white church slid softly by
Scarcely seen by the musing eye.
The few little towns seemed hardly real,
Toy hamlets one could see and feel
As a dreamer would. And the endless road,
Like a river, beneath us smoothly flowed.
Then a slowing pace and a sudden glare—
The lights of the city. We were there,
Slowly we roused ourselves to creep
Gropingly back from enchanted sleep.

L. F. K.

Rue

I have come back to the house of my fathers,
Wide crumbling gates mark the long avenue.
Dark-spreading oaks hold but shadowy welcome.
Was it *right* to have come? Is this what I should do?

Watery sunlight makes flickering shadows,
Tears wet the grass from the night's heavy dew.
There is the tangled and overgrown garden,
Planted with rosemary, roses,—and rue.

The ancient gray house is sagging and broken:
Doorsills are rotting, the shutters awry.
From under moss-covered eaves comes a whisper,
Reproachful and bitter, a heart-broken cry:

Why have you come, now it no longer matters?
Now on my roof-tree the heavy years lie,—
Forsaken, deserted, my family scattered,
Loveless, forgotten, I'm waiting to die.

Back down the avenue, blindly I stumble,
Like a dead leaf by an autumn wind blown,—
Ache in my heart for my lost drifting people,
Grief for the old house left dying alone.

L. F. K.

42

Lost

I know the road, it was just here.
It led,—oh yes, I do know where—
But wait,—this isn't right;
By now the house should be in sight
Beyond those trees. It must be near.
But still, I see it isn't there.
We used to come this way at night,
Always we could see a light.
I knew the road.

E. V. H.

Midnight

on

Water

Street

Caterwauling in the night.
Mist drifts through the saline air
Wispy in the eerie light.
    (caterwauling)

A shadow moves there on the wall
Blacker than soot-laden leaves;
I see no movement now at all.
    (caterwauling)

The street-light flickers dimly here,
Phosphorus eyes gleam in the dark.
A crouching form is hidden there.
    (caterwauling)

E. V. H.

*On
the
Battery*

I had forgotten how the underside
Of tables look when you're almost as tall
As people's hands, and how the rugs and all
The cracks in floors and mouldings do provide
For tracks and streets; and what a pleasant ride
A shoulder gives; how nasty is a fall
And getting clean; and I could not recall
What mysteries they are that grown-ups hide,
Until I saw him solemnly explore
The ribs of a dead leaf. Once, then again
He'd drop it; puzzled, pick it up once more.
Such funny, foreign truck to one whose brain,
For all his eighteen months, just could not know
That leaves had been like that a year ago.

E. V. H.

Down on the Battery
In a sing-song
Children are playing
'Send 'em along.'

Send
'em
Along

Dahs on the benches
Chat all day
Seeing the children
Are safe at play.

Up on the monument
One child stands,
Faces the others
And then demands:
Children come home!
But the children won't come.

If you don't come I'll . . .
Send a cop
After you!

Send 'em along!

If you don't come I'll . . .
Send a tree
After you!

But the children won't come.

If you don't come I'll . . .
Send a boat
After you!

Send 'em along!

If you don't come I'll . . .
Send a witch
After you!

Send 'em along!

If you don't come I'll . . .
Send a switch
After you!

Send 'em along!

If you don't come I'll . . .
Send an elf
After you!

Send 'em along!

Then after a while
Comes the expected
Change in the patter
Children, children, what's the matter?
If you don't come I'll
Send MY SELF
After you!

And then without any more ado
All the children
Scatter.

E. V. H.

Jasper, Jasper, time out of mind,
Let's do a very fast jump rope rhyme:
Run from the Battery

Jump   Up to the Green;

Rope   Trip down King Street;

Chant I   Skip down Queen.
Blow down East Bay.
What do you mean?
That's right, Baby,
One at a time.
This is the end of the
Jump rope rhyme.

E. V. H.

48

Jump
Rope
Chant II

Grandmother Virginia, Grandmother Lish,
Hopping John is a very fine dish.
Grandfather David and Grandfather Louis,
Chinese Dawson hates chop suey.
My Aunt Lucy and your Uncle Moose,
Who did you say shot the wild goose?
Grandmother Beth and Great-aunt Betty,
Round the world in a whirl of confetti.
Great-aunt Beck and Uncle Tom,
Come on girls, dance up a storm!
Uncle Stuart and Aunt May,
We have great–grand aunts, they say.
Uncle Jack, Cracker Jack!
(Run to the Battery, don't come back.)
Mother! Daddy!
Baby Sister!
That's all MISTER!

E. V. H.

Meeting
Street

We Charlestonians
Like to meet
On the street.
We like to think
Ours is a friendly city
And we pity
Those Bostonians
Who blink
Disdainfully or painfully
When they pass a fellow citizen
On the street.
We enjoy one another.
We even greet a stranger like a brother.

And it is the truth:
Youth's polite to age
And age to youth.

Why, we remember—
A trifling thing,
And yet significant:
On Meeting Street
One day
Seeing good Dr. Kershaw, the august—
Rector of St. Michael's,
White thatched, and all of that—
Return the greeting of a little colored boy,
Who'd deferentially doffed his cap,
And heard him say,
A gay
Good Morning, John,
While ceremoniously
Taking off his hat.   H. AND K.

Down Savage Street

Down Savage Street to Chisolm's Mill,
Grandfather's hand in mine,
I danced toward high adventure.
All the houses seemed to shine.
A special magic in the sun
Gave me enchanted eyes.
Grandfather also seemed to feel
The wonder and surprise.
The city's border was a wall,
Where Tradd and Savage meet,
And I released Grandfather's hand
To skip across the street
And see, below, my happy face
Reflected in the sea.
Grandfather's wavy image, too,
Was smiling back at me.
At Chisolm's Mill, Grandfather said,
While giving me his hand,
You'll spend a busy morning, Toots,
Ecstatic in the sand.

L. F. K.

William
Motte,
Butler
and
Diplomat

Now here is charm,
The kind you hope to meet and seldom do;
And here is courtesy
Which makes you feel important that you're you.
His graceful tact
And unforced laughter flatteringly endue
The dullest jest
With sprightly humor that is fresh and new.

L. F. K.

Garden Party

A Botticelli maiden
In flowered gown
Talks to another
From out of town.
Gazebo and pergola,
With roses laden;
Paths neatly raked,
Delphinium staked
In prim array,
In bloom today.

And from within
A happy din
Intensified
By polished surfaces inside.
Dark floors gleaming,
Hostess beaming,
Little old ladies
Wining,
Dining.

The silver epergne's filled with flowers,
Why she must have worked for hours!
Delicious dainties—many choices.
And buzzing all around
The cheerful sound
Of Charleston voices.

That little wizened person, there,
Lives only on this party fare.
(That's why she's shrunk so very small).
Now, pulling down her stays,
She's up to her old ways:
Important, standing very tall,
She breasts the biggest debutante of all,
And, flinching, we can hear:
My, how you've GROWN, my dear!

Surreptitiously,
But deliciously,
Another old lady filches the cakes,
So she can give a party, too,
Since her stove no longer bakes.

And over there
Seated in the drawing room,
Eight octogenarians bloom,—
While William Motte serves champagne—
Living their debutante days again.

E. V. H.

Dah

My black dah
From the depths of her full heart
Croons minor melodies.
Hymns they are to the white man's God
But sung as no white man can sing them.
Her voice is like
Blue smoke rising upward
Through the haze
Of the deep pine forest.
No barbarism this;
That's long forgot.
These notes bear impress
Of that plaintive quietude
That breathes around Dah's home.
The hush of hidden sanctuary
Deep in the cypress swamp,
The windblown marsh,
The smudge of trees
Where the herons nest,
And the deep blue sky
Where one lone blackbird
Circles with indolent grace.

E. V. H.

Dah died.
I needed her and went to find her
And called her name.

Dah

Died

    Lucille Davis
    Is she here?

    She dead,
Some ragged children said.
Her geraniums still stood
In their rusty cans
On the rail of the porch upstairs.
Then a woman came to the slanting door.
    Two, three weeks ago.
    And no one let me know?
    No ma'am. She dead.

    Her children?
    Oh, they moved.

Dah's children!
The one who had fallen on her head
And kept the boys out of school,
    they have to watch her
    she lacking sense.
The one who had a baby at fourteen,
    so I can't git no welfare.

56

Instead, I saw
The poverty as mine
Not Dah's.
I saw my brittle and acquisitive life
And understood
Humans are not made great
Collecting Meissen figurines in a row,
Whatever their perfection.

E. V. H.

Nameless God says they're His kids
But of course, you know
We're a lot better than God
And we can't fool with them.

E. V. H.

Hypocrite

How does it feel, being a hypocrite?
Do you lick your tongue around your lips
And cringe and smile—on purpose?
And know that you are vile and slimy—
Or do you think that you are good and sound
And shut your eyes and call yourself benevolent
And tell The Lord that you and He
Are the only two in all the universe
Who know what goodness is?
And then, when you've done that,
Do you not
Suspect yourself a little tiny bit?
And how do you feel then?

E. V. H.

Mrs. A

Mrs. A
Had a black moustache
And straggly hair,
A very dark face,
(at least in the creases).
It may have come
From not washing
Or black despair.
Her husband, we heard,
And her sons as well,
Were not above raising
Considerable hell.
Without a doubt
They left her out.
Her days were spent
On a special bent,
Searching out ancestors' lives
In dusty, musty dim archives.

It used to make me very sad
Thinking of the life she had
But now I think she was upheld
By the way she dug and delved.
The past gave her its rich rewards
Though the present
Was unpleasant.

E. V. H.

Mrs. B

First Mr. B's estate ran out,
Then Mr. B just died,
Leaving Mrs. B about
Just nothing but her pride.

A tea-room did she condescend
To open in her rooms,
And likewise, her poor fortunes mend
By selling off heirlooms.

She cluttered up her little space
With candlesticks and chairs,
A little Spode, a little lace,
All sold with little airs.

When gentle customers came in
And ordered tea and toast,
Mrs. B allowed them ample time
To see what they liked most.

But Mrs. B still had her pride!
One liked the chandelier
And asked the price, and said aside,
It's quite a find, my dear!

The chandelier! cried Mrs. B
(Her anger made them quail).
*That chandelier belongs to me
And it is not for sale!*

*Why that is what the Spanish king
Bestowed on Grandpa Tate.
Why that's the most insulting thing!
Good day! There is the gate!*

E. V. H.

My
House
and
I

My little house, it sags in the middle
Like the loosened string of a worn-out fiddle;
The plaster falls, and the woodwork's peeling,
The paper threatens to leave the ceiling,
And I think a mouse
Lives in my house.

My little house is in need of painting,
Some of its boards, decay is tainting;
And once in the night was a sound appalling,
Noise of bricks in the chimney falling;
The hard rains douse
My little house.

When hurricanes roar, the salt waves, curling
Over the porch of my house come purling
In foaming rage, and retire snarling—
Baffled, too, for my house, the darling,
Though a drunken house,
Is a cheerful souse.

It shakes itself, when the storm is finished,
Smiles with a gaiety undiminished;
For a hundred years it has laughed at weather—
Now I am here, and we laugh together—
How we carouse,
Me and my house!

L. F. K.

My Tenant

I have a house within my house,
My tenant is a small gray mouse;
And Dick says we must set a trap
With jaws that close with ringing snap
To catch my tenant and put him out.
Dick says what am I thinking about
To let a mouse
Live in the house!

But he looks so soft and he's awfully small,
He doesn't get in the way at all,—
Doesn't interrupt when we are speaking;
I've never even heard him squeaking.
And he eats so little, a piece of bread
Or sometimes cracker crumbs instead.
And he wipes his feet.
He's very neat.

He used to skitter across the floor
But he isn't afraid of me any more,—
Just goes on happily with his chewing
Or whatever else it is he's doing.
Dick says set a trap with cheese to bait him
And very quickly exterminate him.
I suppose I should,—
But I never could.

L. F. K.

Gentle

Ghost

A phantom lady walks my rooms.
How many houses here can boast
A spirit crowned with scented blooms
Like my own smiling little ghost?

Sometimes at night, in lonely dark,
I feel the faint slow rise of fear;
Then comes her gentle whisper, *Hark!*
You mustn't be afraid. I'm here!

When she was living here, her charm
So permeated rooms and halls
That they retain it still. No harm
Could enter these enchanted walls.

As some old-fashioned potpourri
Perfumes a room and lingers there,
The joy that she bequeathed to me
Lives in the laughter-haunted air.

L. F. K.

She
Haunts
the
Dock
Street
Theatre

She wore a bustle
Did Miss Burdell
And lived for years
In the Planters Hotel.
The Planters Hotel
Was a dreadful place.
It was, in fact,
A civic disgrace
(Until it was changed
By the WPA
Into the theater of today.
You know that the Dock Street Theater is
The Planters Hotel's metamorphosis.)
But for Miss Burdell
There were no repairs.
Her room was up
Three flights of stairs;
The plaster fell
From rain or rot;
She may have had water
But probably not.
The City Council
Might have had pity
For indigent ladies
Filled the city
But, chances are
It was turned off till
Somebody had paid
The water bill.

But who took care of her
No one knew;
She sat in church
In a paid-for pew;
Refused the bounty
Of Ladies' Aid
With pride intact,
Though gloves were frayed.
Under St. Michael's portico,
Walking with mincing steps,
She'd go.
Tourists who saw her
Said, *How Quaint!*
Mannerly children
Showed restraint.
Her hats, her guimpes
Her stays, her veils
Are part and parcel
Of our folk tales.

In fact, it was
All over town
She once called
Dr. Rutledge down!
He was talking
To some men,—
She passed
And then came back again.

Impossible!
He'd failed to speak!
Her attitude
Was far from meek!
Her words, indeed,
Were somewhat shady,
One marvelled at them
From a lady.

When they demolished
The old hotel,
Everyone worried
For Miss Burdell.
The story we heard
Was: she was taken
Up to Columbia,
Not forsaken.
But—certainly not
Of her own accord—
She was installed
In a mental ward.
Her hat was firmly
Pinned to her head;
She wouldn't undress
Nor go to bed,
Nor let a doctor anywhere near.
Some called it pride,
But others fear.

Then Dr. Milling,
Both kind and wise
Looked at the problem
Through her eyes.
He thereupon renamed his staff
And cautioned them:—
They mustn't laugh.

I beg you, ma'am,
Don't be upset
Your nurse, here,
Is Miss Prioleau Rhett.
If you need something
Simply call
The maid, whose name
Is Gaillard Ball.
You are among friends,
Dear Miss Burdell
Here's Dr. Rutledge Huger Ravenel!

E. V. H.

Remodeled
Kitchen
House

On Wednesday noon the plumber came
(He *said* he'd be there Monday),
And took the bathroom fixtures out
And left them over Sunday.
He then removed the ancient pipes,
Replacing them *en masse*,
But, underneath the kitchen, he
Did something to the gas.
We telephoned the Gas Repair
To come and fix the leak.
Meanwhile, the plumber left and then
The tile men came next week.
We told them we expected guests
A short ten days away;
They promised they would do their best
To finish in a day.
True to their word, they hurried on,
The work progressed apace.
They left. Alas! Beside the door
They also left a space
Which should have had three tiles therein.
Two days elapsed. They came,
Installed the tiles and threw cement
Down in the bathtub drain.
New fixtures now the plumber brought,
Installed them, then was fain
To open up the box behind
The tub and clear the drain.

Now this, in turn, necessitates
A carpenter's repairs,
So we procured a carpenter
Who fixed the box and shares
The credit for its beauty with
The painter who restored
The finish it had formerly.
I hope you are not bored,
Because I'm forced to tell you that
You haven't heard the end!
Somehow the carpenter had knocked
A hole. We had to send
To get the plumber back again
To plug the leaking pipe.
Self-pity is degrading
And I really shouldn't gripe,
But I am going to take a trip
Up to the Bay of Fundy
And well and truly drown myself,
If he's not here on Monday.

L. F. K.

Early
Spring

Come, let us walk in Hampton Park on a cool and
    hazy morning;
We'll come upon a flock of ducks without a quack of
    warning
And see azaleas' waking buds while Spring is still
    a-borning.
Beneath the gray of misty clouds and sky of wrinkled
    satin,
The soft and vagrant little winds uplift the leaves,
    and flatten
The grasses briefly as they pass to sing a gentle matin.
This morning, in its minor key, is something we'll
    remember,
The silver tones, the waking buds as soft as glowing
    ember,
Through budding May and burning June, on into
    dim December.

L. F. K.

And
While
Ye
May,
Go
Marry

Accept your lover, do not plan and wait
Until you have collected all that bale
Of comforts sixty years requires for its pale
Thin humors. Do not load your youth with freight
You buy too dearly. See, before too late
A palace—furnished—is not worth the sale
Of one half-hour you're losing of the gale
Of stirring April's power to consummate.
Accept your lover, when the blowing wind
Shall rush along the rooftree do not sleep
Alone in purple darkness with unkind
And sterile sheets for covering and keep
Your mind chastized and ecstacy at bay.
Accept your lover: April does not stay.

E. V. H.

The fog horns wake me in the night
And in the shrouded gloom
I hear the city speak:

I
Heard
the
City
Speak

Gnawed by rodent people
Who walk my ancient streets,
I gape in agony.
I have been a proud city in my day,
Proud of my port
Which served the world.
Proud of my courteous citizens,
Teachers and librarians,
Artists and historians;
Proud of stately buildings and small parks,
Of measured coigns,
Poetic ironwork,
Proud of my houses
Of bricks well-laid in Flemish bond,
Plum-colored tile,
Chimney pots and mockingbirds,
Of single dwellings, tall and functional,
Of shuttered windows, wide piazzas
Built to catch the uncontaminated air.
Proud of wooden houses, large and small,
Their gable ends towards the street,
Their gates ensuring privacy.

Harmony of brick and tile,
Harmony of plan and style,
Rhythm of indented gables,
Georgian houses, gothic stables.
Little houses made of wood,
Unpretentious they have stood
Each in scale and in proportion.

A whole row
(humble but mine own)
Disappeared on Meeting Street the other day,
Unnoticed.

A fringe of lonely structures
Might be preserved;
While a block of high brick walls and hidden ways
Is gutted for a parking lot.
A stage set—
Not a city.

Petitions flying,
Tempers rising,
A few defenders put their fingers in the dyke
To stop a demolition here,
A modernizing there.
But the picture is destroyed,
Sacrificed to shining motor cars
Which scuttle, in their hard shells
About my streets
And are worshipped
By my inhabitants.

A bulldozed highway slashes here
And alien beautifiers are called in
To sanctify the scar.
There, a store, like an apron,
Spreads across a chaste facade
To serve a neighborhood
And sell fat-back and collard greens;
While down the street
A tall house huddles
Against a giant oak,
Both doomed.

I am become a leprous and amorphous thing.

The incoming traveller
No more is greeted by golden marshes,
Swinging with red-winged blackbirds,
Opening vistas to the sea;—
Or moss-hung savannahs where white herons fly.
Slash pine will never form a colonnade
Down a lonely road.
Only choked garbage, dumped,
And littered roadsides
Smeared with oil,
Strung with ugly wires,
Lined with garish billboards,
Bid him welcome.
The seven-hundred-year-old oak,
Laid low to make a concrete drive-in,
Will not grow again.
This might be some desert town,
Scratching its bare existence in a hostile land.

And yet—
On sunny days,
The North wind brushes clean
The opaque air,
Then aureate light plays on classic balustrades
And banana trees drip shadows on a wall,

> *In places*
> *I am Charleston still.*
> *The signs of greatness that fashioned me*
> *into a city,*
> *Not a town,*
> *Remain.*

Some rows of houses still survive,
Neighborhoods that clean their faces,
Not only in self-conscious patches
But in unexpected places.

Here, too, are my own true people,
Belonging like St. Michael's Steeple.
My stevedore unloads the ships;
My little fitter sews and rips;
My bricklayer toils in dusty clothes;
My ancient beggar comes and goes;
My shrimp vendor cries his wares;
My shrewd housewife shops, compares;
My gardener prunes and clips the grass;
My prim housemaid shines the brass;
My children play their time-worn games
On the streets with old French names.

A master carpenter once said in pity
Of his friend who left the city:
'As for me, I've got it made,
I myself, I would not trade
Three states, for this one city.'

My old roots will bear again.
Flowers form in winter's rain.
Camellias are pruned to thrive.
I am Charleston, and alive.
As fog and wind and beating rain,
Changes come but I remain.

E. V. H.

77